Ready Made Tour Brain

Billie Jo Cavallaro

CONTENTS:
18 POLAROIDS
OF A READY MADE TOUR BRAIN

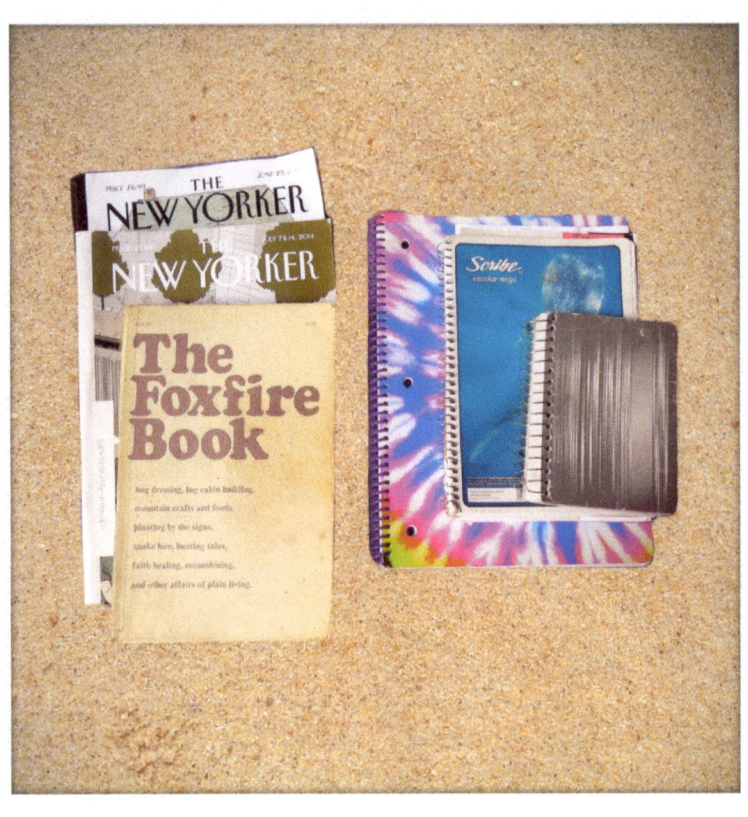

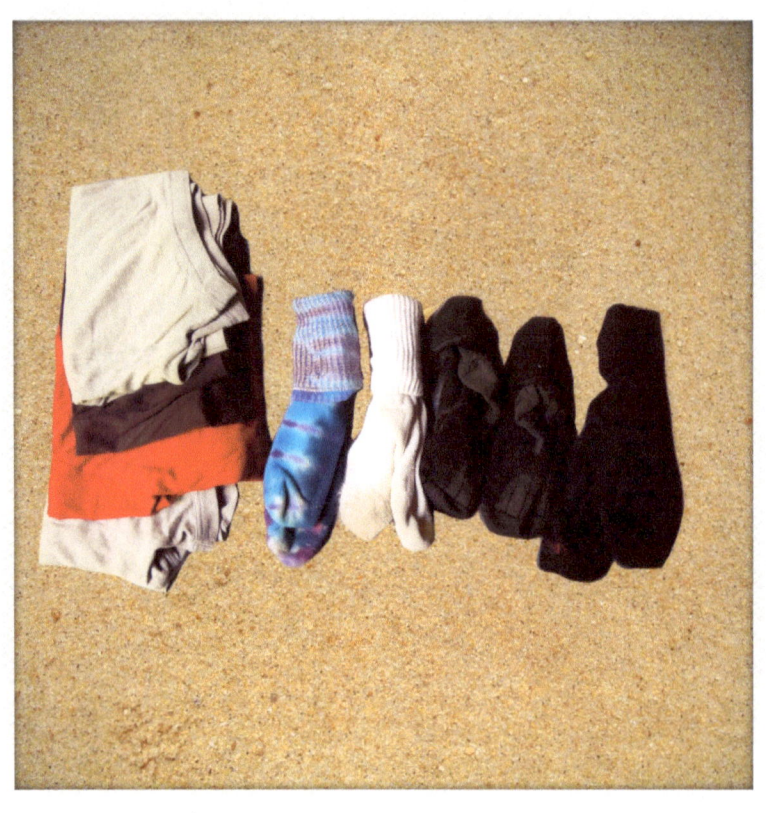

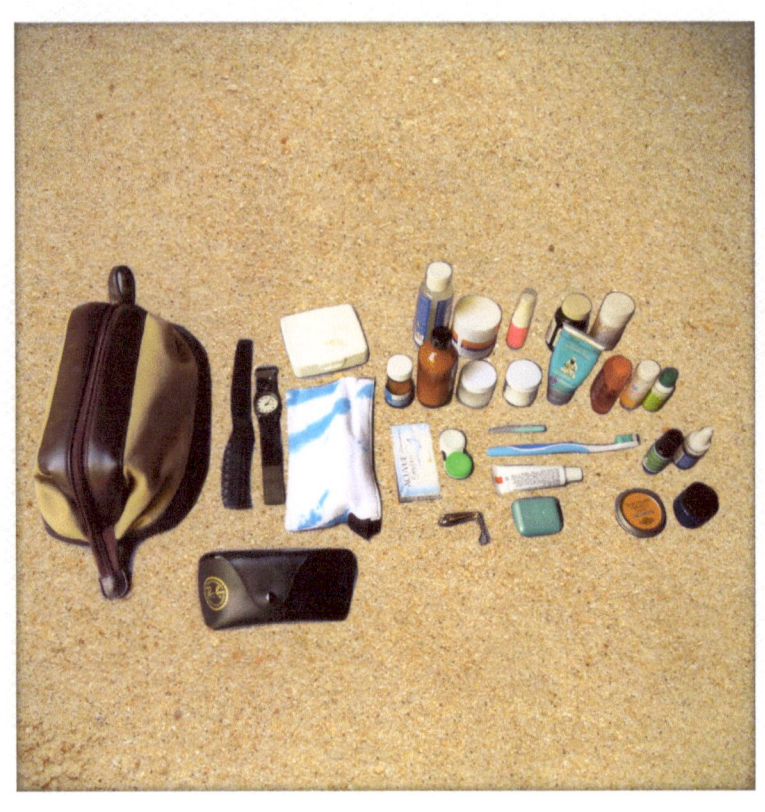

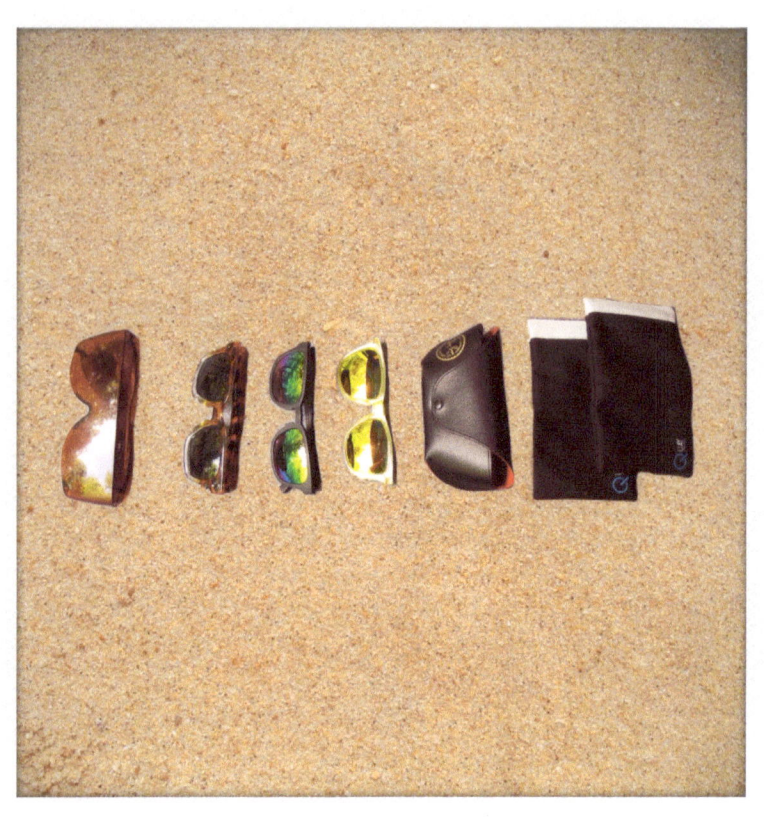

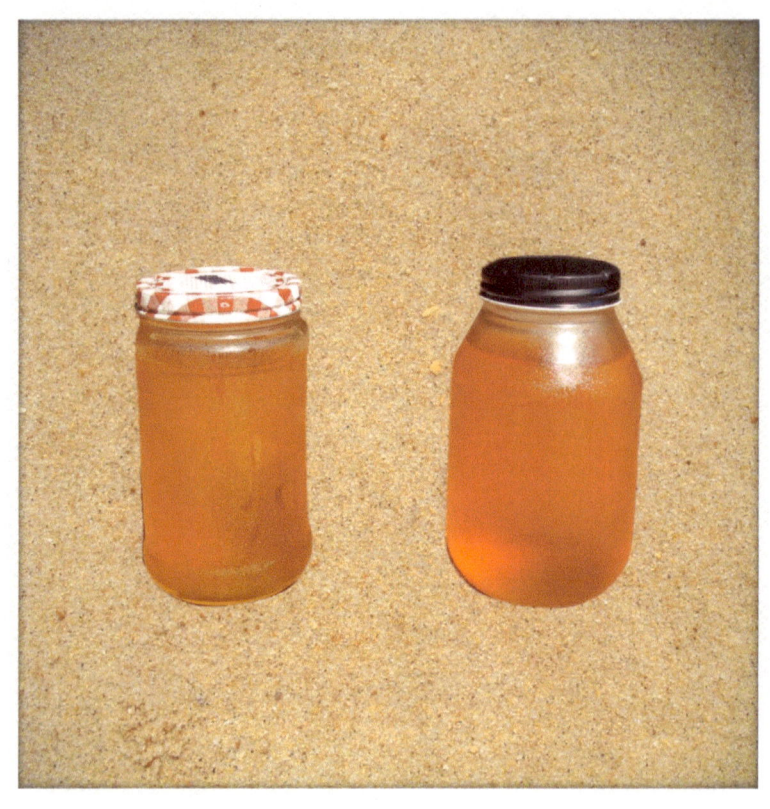

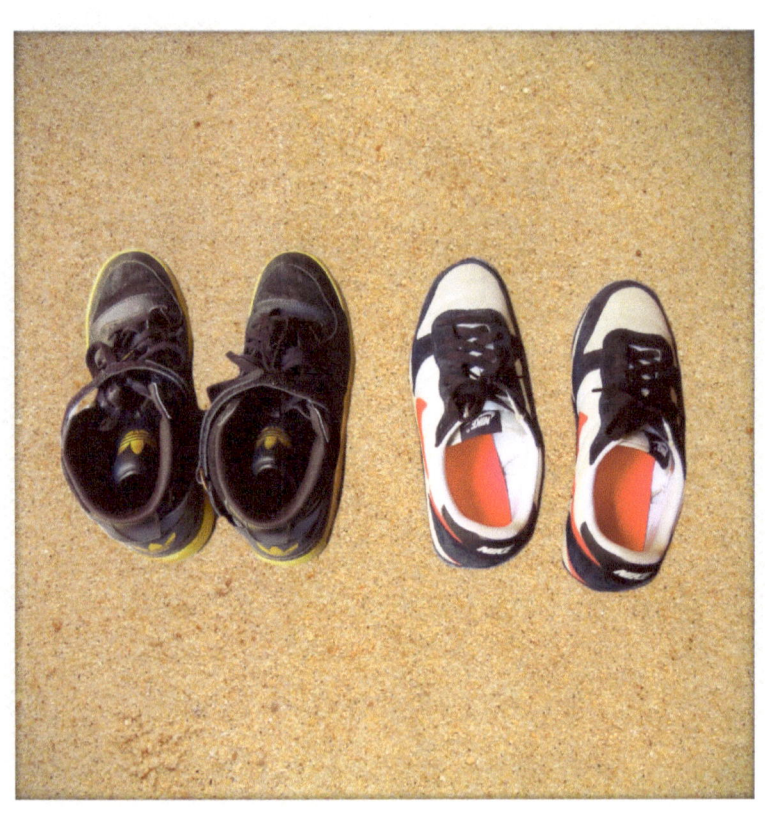

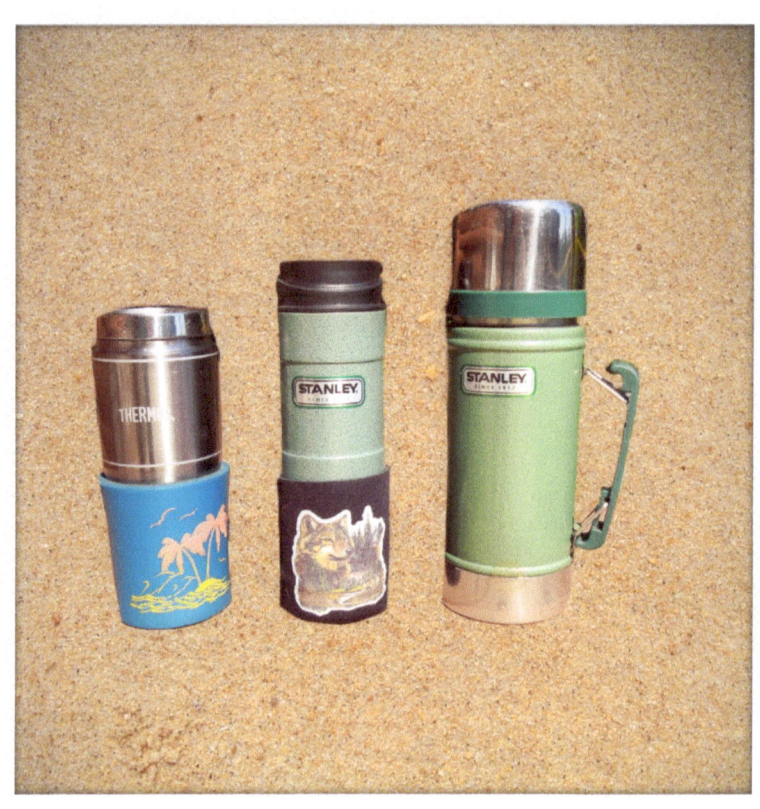

14

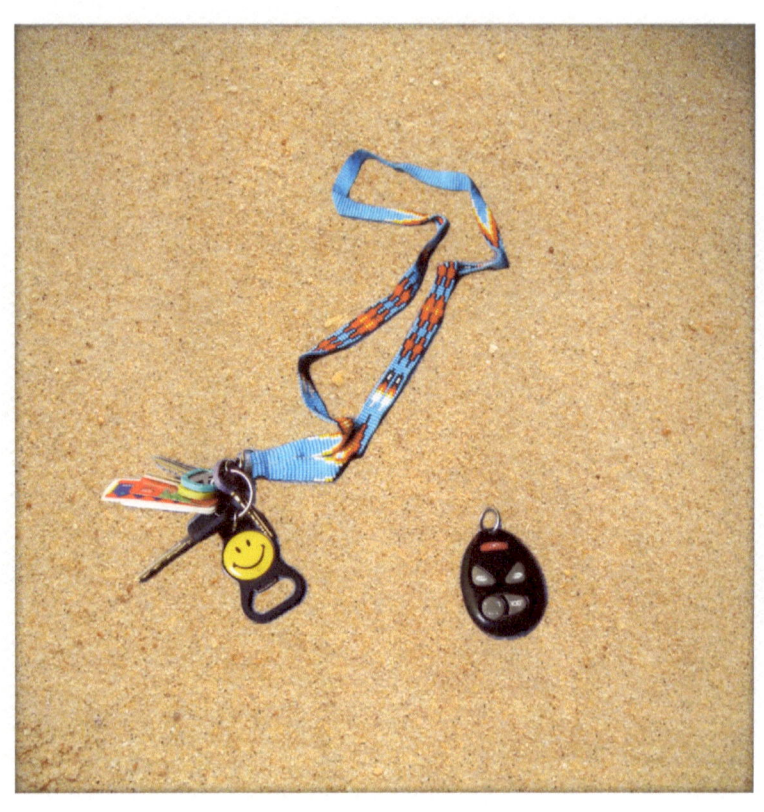

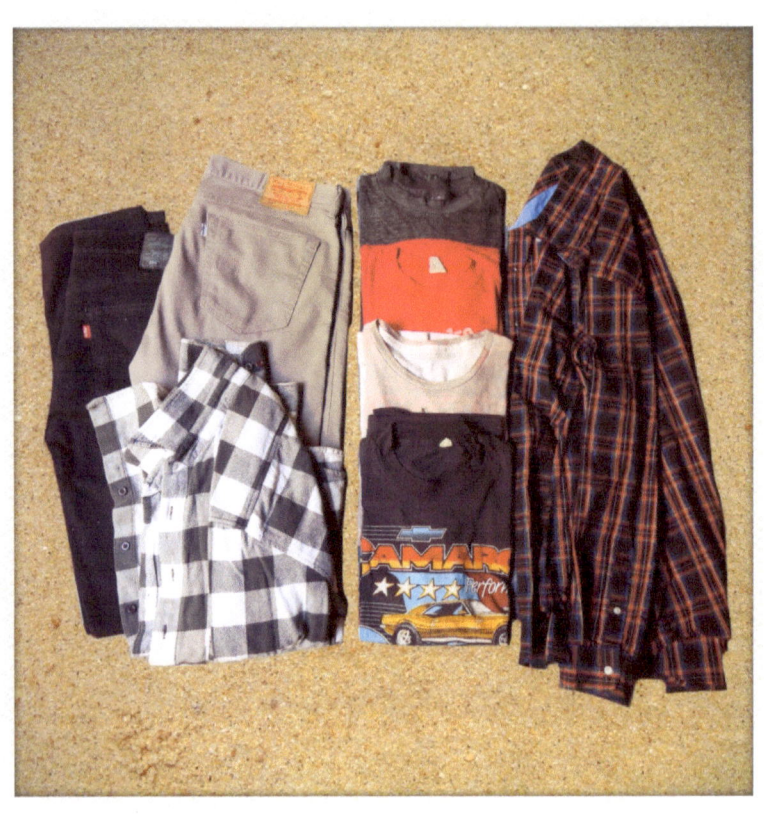

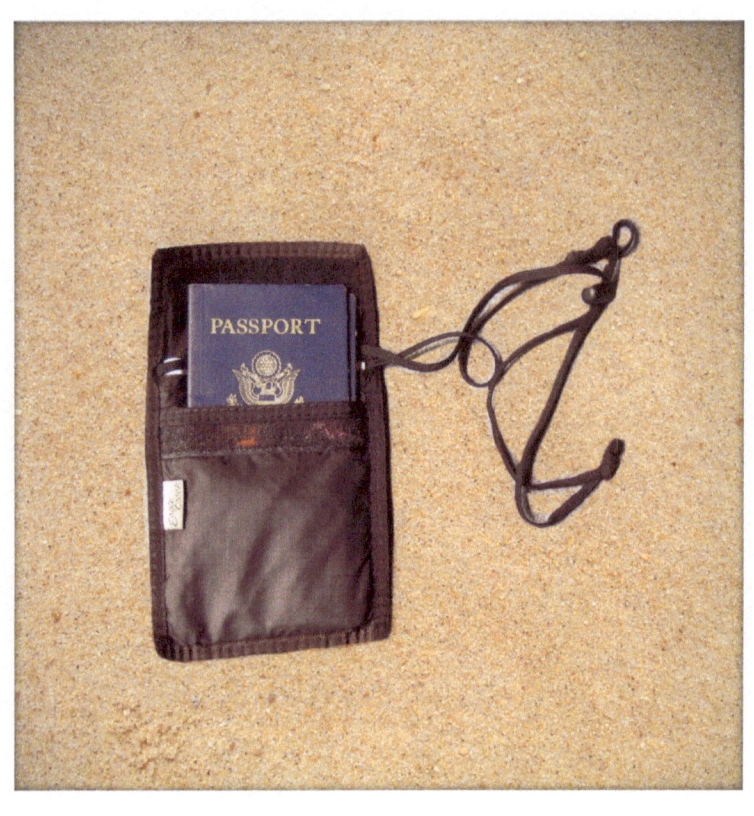

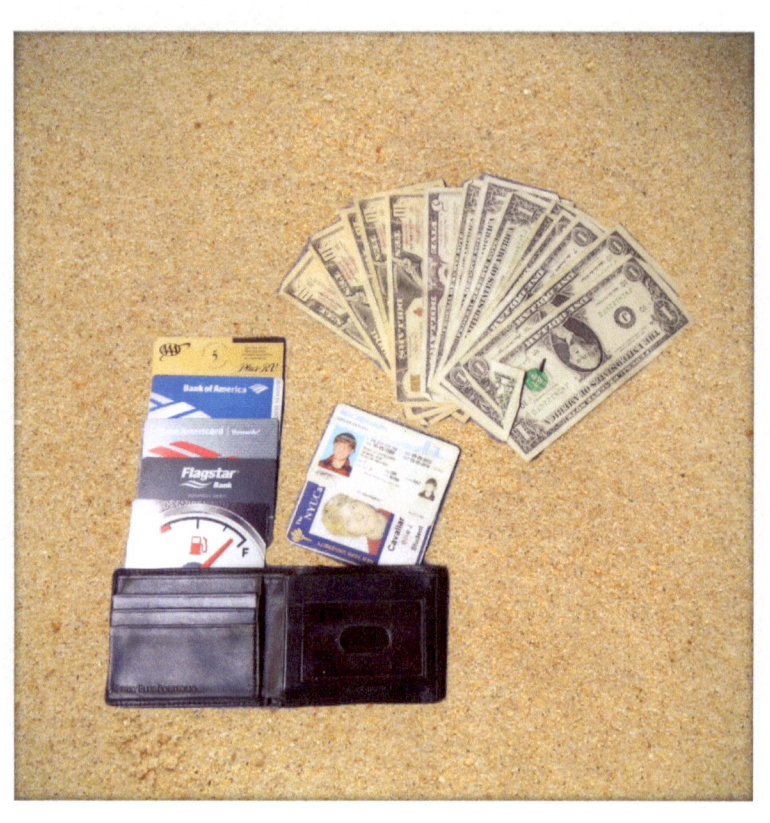

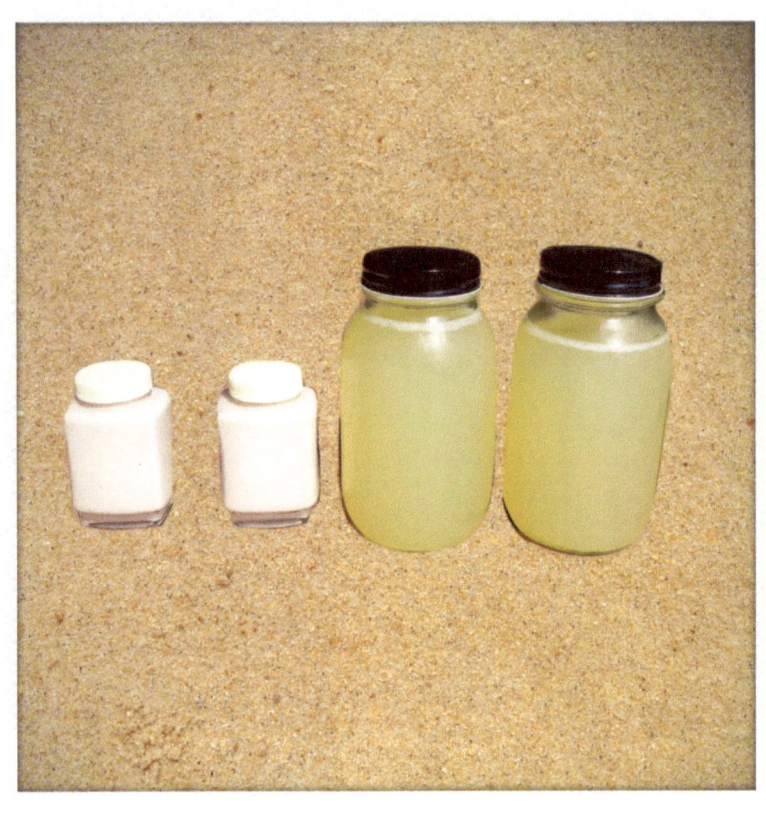

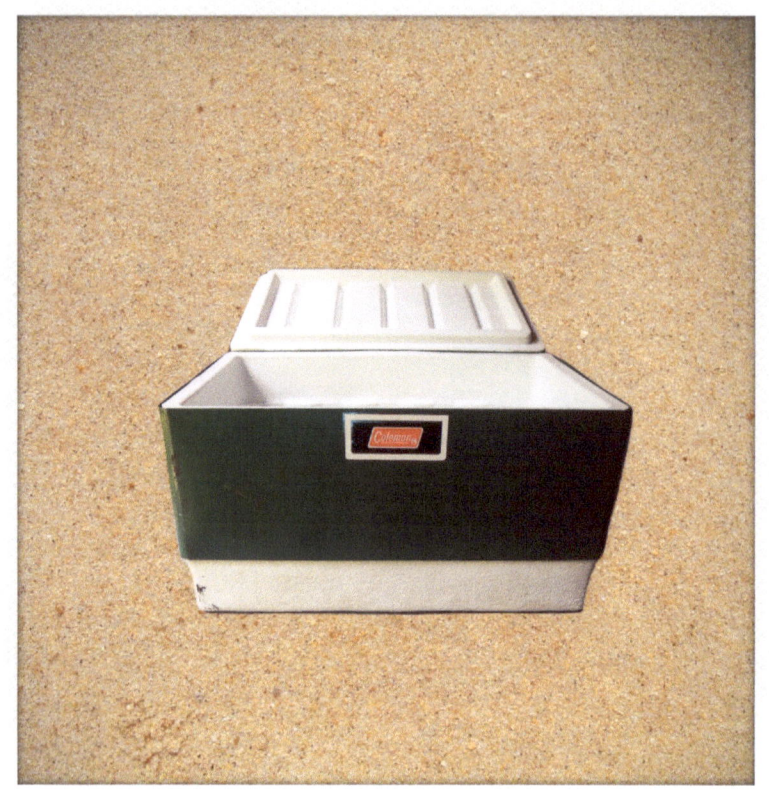

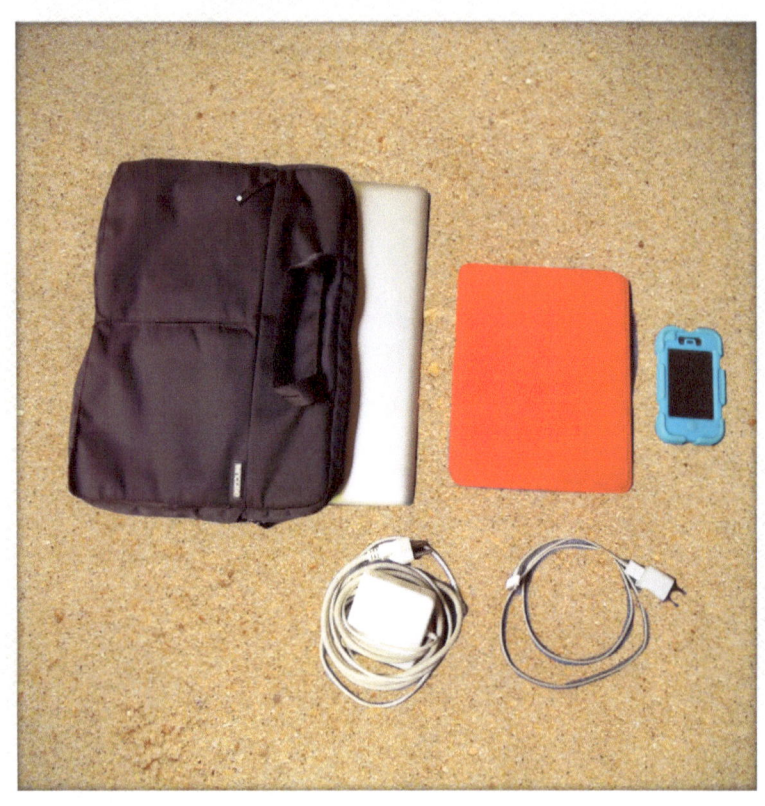

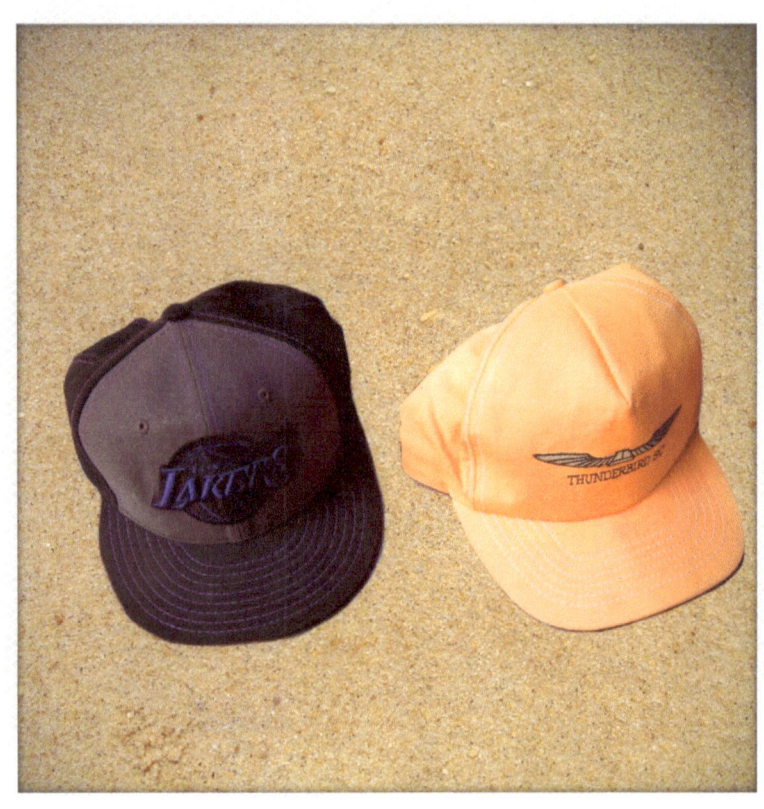

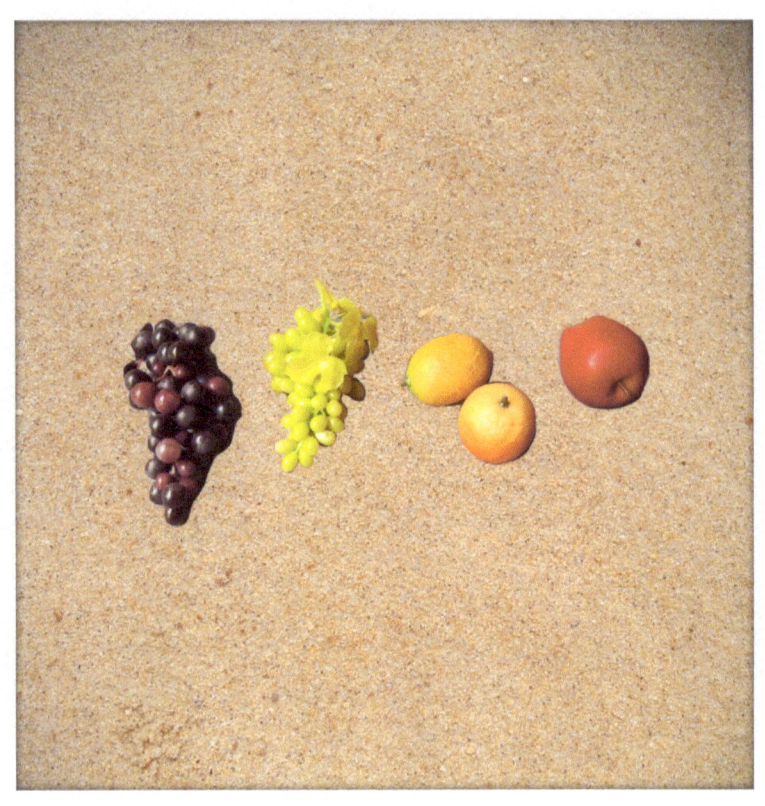

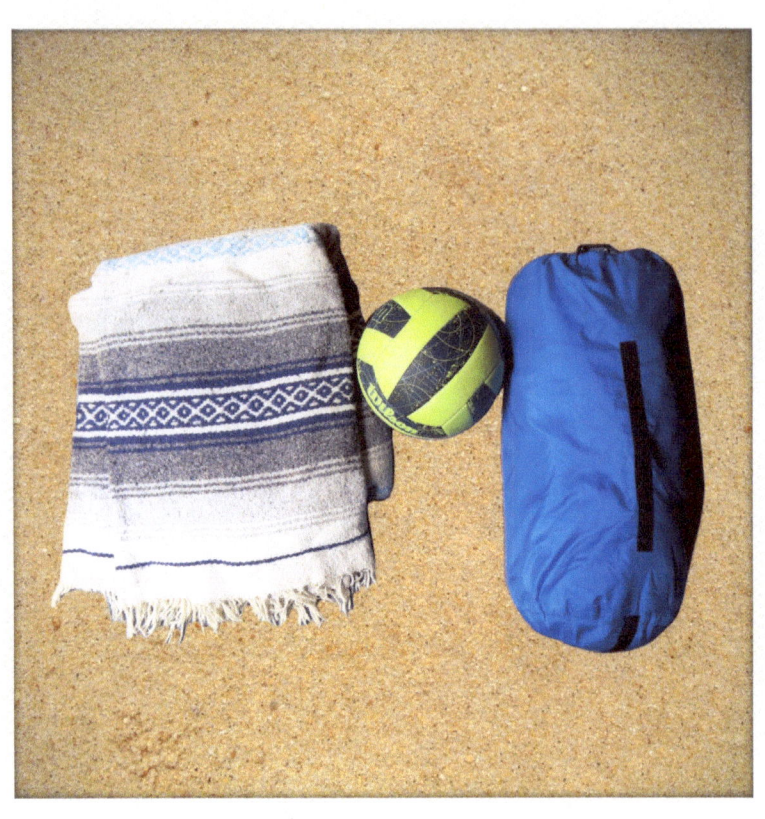

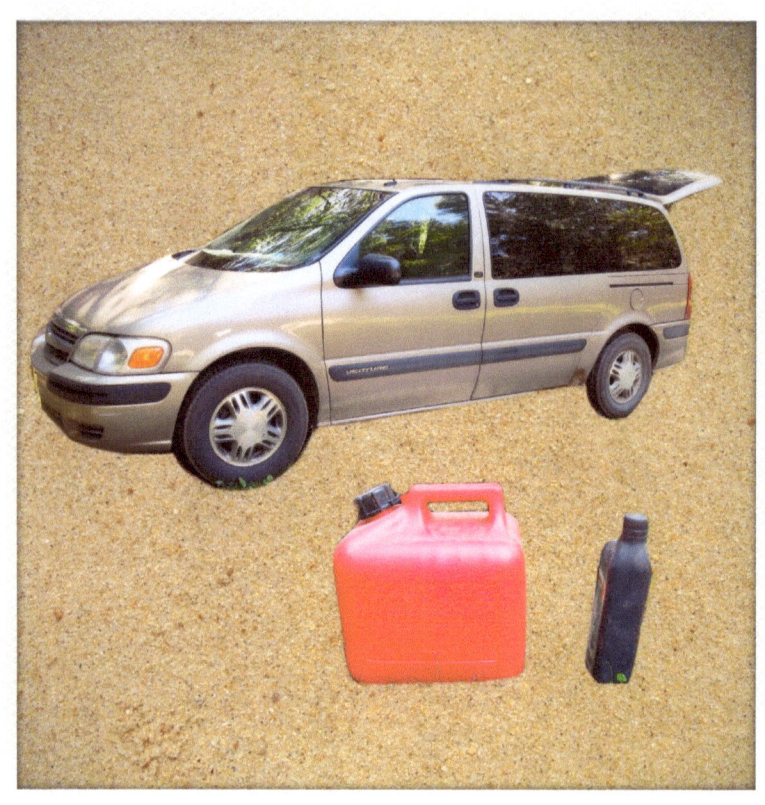

BILLIE JO CAVALLARO
BORN 1980
GRADUATED WMU 2003
GRADUATED NYU 2008

LOS ANGELES BASED CONCEPTUAL ARTIST,
WORKING IN VIDEO, PHOTO, SCULPTURE, AND
INSTALLATION.

www.ingramcontent.com/pod-product-compliance
Lightning Source LLC
Chambersburg PA
CBHW040927180526
45159CB00002BA/644